The Two Main Sources of Marie de l'Incarnation's Prayer

Fr. Michel LEGAULT, M.S.A.

En Route Books and Media, LLC

St. Louis, MO

⊕*ENROUTE*
Make the time

En Route Books and Media, LLC
5705 Rhodes Avenue
St. Louis, MO 63109

Cover credit: Sebastian Mahfood, from oil painting attributed to Hughes Pommier

ISBN-13: 978-1-952464-82-9

Table of Contents

Introduction

On October 28, 1999, the Catholic Church celebrated the 400th anniversary of the birth of Marie Guyard, known now as Saint Marie de l'Incarnation (canonized 3 April 2014 at the Apostolic Palace by Pope Francis), "*The Teresa of the New World.*"[1] I wish this simple research on Marie de l'Incarnation's prayer (conducted in 1999) to be considered as an act of admiration and gratitude to God the Father who made this humble woman a luminous witness of His love in the

---

[1] Maria-Paul del Rosario Adriazola, *La connaissance sprituelle chez Marie de l'Incarnation*, Paris, Les Editions du Cerf, 1989, p. 377.

1

beginning of the Church in North America. At the present time, the *New Age* is searching for new ways of knowledge to reach God. Why does one search in esoterism for the path to God? Marie Guyard, even when she was seven years old, already knew the path to God the Father: this path for her was Jesus whom she met in the Church, who spoke to her in the Scripture, who united her to himself in the Eucharist, and who taught her the divine mysteries through the action of the Holy Spirit.

What were the lines of force of Marie Guyard's prayer? How did she nourish it while working for her brother-in-law[2] on the docks[3] of

---

[2] A. Fournet, "Marie de l'Incarnation", in *Catholic Encyclopedia*. Tran-

Tours as well as teaching Algonquin

---

scribed by Douglas J. Potter. Encyclopedia Press, Inc., Electronic version,
1977. At the age of 17, in obedience to
her parents, Marie Guyard married
Claude Martin, a silk manufacturer of
Tours. They had a son who was also
called Claude; became a Benedictine
priest in the Order of *Saint-Maur*. Her
husband died after two years of married life. When her son reached the age
of twelve, she entered the Ursuline Order in Tours and went to Canada in
1639 to found a school for the educa-
tion of Indian and French girls. She
died at Quebec, April 30, 1672.

[3] Her brother-in-law placed Marie
in charge of his business, which was a
large transport and warehouse compa-
ny. She had to spend the day and often
the night among porters, carters, and
horses. At times, she was still on the
wharf at midnight, loading and un-
loading goods. Cf. Fernand Jetté, *The
Spiritual Teaching of Mary of the Incarnation*, p. 72.

and French girls in the early years of Quebec City? What are the pillars of her contemplative and apostolic life?

It is to answer those questions that I chose to reflect on the foundations of Marie de l'Incarnation's prayer. With what spiritual food did she feed her prayer and her intimate union with God? After having read her letters and some commentaries on her spirituality, I think I can underline two important sources:[4]

---

[4] Maria-Paul del Rosario Adrazola, in *La connaissance spirituelle chez Marie de l'Incarnation*, on p. 260, writes the following lines which confirm my first intuition: "Pour Marie de l'Incarnation la Bible est, avec l'Eucharistie, source de sa connaissance—contact avec le Dieu vivant, et moyen de réponse et d'expression." ["For Mary of the Incarnation the Bible is, along with

first, the Word of God, speaking in **Holy Scripture**. Second, the sacraments, especially the Eucharist, that Jesus entrusted to his Church to give the life of grace and which are celebrated in the sacred **Liturgy, the prayer of the Church**. From these two sources - Holy Scripture and Liturgy - I will briefly show how they influenced Marie de l'Incarnation's spiritual life, as well as being the sources of each Christian's life of prayer.

---

the Eucharist, the source of her knowledge—contact with the living God, and a means of response and expression."]

The First Source of Marie de l'Incarnation's Prayer:

Holy Scripture

When I read the writings of Marie de l'Incarnation, I was amazed by the importance of the Holy Scripture in her spiritual life. Even though she never studied theology nor exegesis, Marie was very familiar with Holy Scripture from the time she was a little girl. The spiritual experience of Marie de l'Incarnation was united with the official teaching of the Church. Marie-Paul del Rosario Adriazola, in her deep study of Marie's spirituality, writes:

"La Révélation contenue dans la Sainte Écriture doit être le fondement de la doctrine énoncée dans les écrits des maîtres spirituels, ainsi que la base de différentes dévotions dans l'Église[5]. Or, on est singulièrement frappé par la place que tient la Sainte Écriture dans la vie et l'œuvre de Marie de l'Incarnation; surtout de voir Dieu

---

[5] The Author, on page 259, writes the following footnote: "L'Encyclique *Haurietis Aquas* sur le Sacré-Cœur (15 mai 1956) constitue un exemple sur ce point; elle prouve l'authenticité de la dévotion au Sacré-Cœur par un exposé des sources scripturaires." ["The Encyclical *Haurietis Aquas* on the Sacred Heart (May 15, 1956) is an example on this point; it proves the authenticity of devotion to the Sacred Heart by an exposition of scriptural sources."]

lui parler et la transformer en se servant des textes scripturaires. Le lecteur devient ainsi un témoin de l'efficacité de l'Écriture dans l'épanouissement et dans le rayonnement des mystiques chrétiens."[6]

["The Revelation contained in Sacred Scripture must be the foundation of the doctrine set forth in the writings of the spiritual masters, as well as the basis of various devotions in the Church. Now, we are singularly struck by the place that Sacred Scripture holds in the

---

[6] Maria-Paul del Rosario Adrazola, *La connaissance spirituelle chez Marie de l'Incarnation*, p. 259. [*Spiritual knowledge within Mary of the Incarnation*]

life and work of Mary of the
Incarnation; above all to see
God speak to her and trans-
form her by using scriptural
texts. The reader thus be-
comes a witness to the effec-
tiveness of Scripture in the
development and influence
of Christian mystics."]

Even when she was young, Marie
Guyard recorded in her heart the
passages of the Bible that she heard
during the Liturgy. She liked the
preachers she listened to because
she was told that God spoke
through them. She writes:

"I was too young to understand much of what was said,
except for the stories which I
recounted on my return

home. As I grew older, my instinctive faith, coupled with what I heard of the Divine Word, produced a greater and greater love in me which led me to go to listen to sermons. [...] When I heard this word it seemed that my heart was like a vessel in which this divine word flowed like liquid. This was not my imagination but rather the power of the Spirit of God who himself was in this divine word and who, by a movement of grace, produced this effect in my soul."[7]

---

[7] Marie de l'Incarnation, *The Relation of 1654*, IV, *Selected writings*, Edited by Irene Mahoney, O.S.U., p. 46.

Father Fernand Jetté, O.M.I., in *The Spiritual Teaching of Mary of the Incarnation*, says that, since it is simple and affective, the prayer using the Holy Scripture does not require much reading. "[…] the only kind that Mary recommends or appears to value highly is the reading of the Bible especially the Psalms and the Gospels."[8] When Mary was young, she already knew the Gospel and the Psalms. The passages of the Bible that she heard in her parish church nourished her dialogue with God. Long before her entry into religious life, Marie had discovered a taste for the Psalms. Marie-Paul del Rosario Adriazola says that the following books of the Bible were the most important in her spiritual life: the *Psalms*, the *Gospels*, espe-

---

[8] Fernand Jetté, *op. cit.*, p. 86.

cially St. John's Gospel, *St. Paul* and the *Song of Songs*.[9] This latter was the best to express her experience of her mystical marriage.

Marie de l'Incarnation knew and loved the Psalms. In October, 1663, she wrote: "I had read the Psalms in French, [...] and in times of need, thoughts and ideas inspired by them would come to me."[10] Father Fernand Jetté recalls: "It was while her soul was filled with a verse of Psalm 30 that she received the grace of her conversion".[11] She was meditating on the line: "*In te domine speravi, non confundar in aeternum.*"

---

[9] Maria-Paul del Rosario Adrazola, *La connaissance spirituelle chez Marie de l'Incarnation*, p. 263.

[10] *Relations of 1654, Écrits*, II. 167, quoted by Fernand Jetté, *op. cit.*, p. 87.

[11] Fernand Jetté, *op. cit.*, p. 86. Cf. *Relation of 1654, Écrits*, II, 167.

In *The Relation of 1654*, Marie de l'Incarnation writes a long passage that demonstrates clearly her love for the Psalms and the use she made of them in her spiritual life. I will quote some excerpts of the letter: she writes:

> "Following the events I have just described which oc-curred about two months af-ter my entrance into reli-gious life, my spirit, still bearing the imprint and unc-tion of this great grace, was more withdrawn than ever from things of earth and drawn toward religious vir-tue and the Divine Office, where Our Lord bestowed on me a sweet and nourishing understanding of Holy Scrip-

ture. While in choir I heard in French what I was chanting in Latin. This so captured my spirit that had I not rigorously controlled myself, this might have been noticeable. The act of singing soothed me and liberated my spirit, so engaging my senses that I had a strong impulse to leap and clap my hands and induce everyone to sing the praises of this great God, so worthy of everyone is being consumed for his love and service and with the bride of the Song "rejoicing and leaping with joy at the remembrance of the embraces of the Spouse." Thus I savored the spirit of these divine words and I would sing the "*Eructavit*" (Psalm 45), proclaiming in inexpressible exuberance the greatness and the prerogatives of my spouse whose words were for me spirit and life."[12]

This passage resembles the attitude we find in St. Teresa of Avila who used to accompany the singing of hymns and canticles with castanets, and also of King David who danced before the Ark of the Covenant. This text shows how the prayer of the Psalms was integrated in the life of Marie de l'Incarnation. Her whole being, soul and body, participated in her prayer of the Psalms. This text should be taught to local Churches which have to

---

[12] Marie de l'Incarnation, *The Relation of 1654*, XXXIV, in Irene Mahoney, *op. cit.*, p. 101.

inculturate the liturgy. While reading this passage, I had the impression they were written by the Black African Nuns who dance and use tom-toms and drums, guitars and *koras* while singing the Psalms. Unfortunately, the joy of the Psalms does not appear in the way the Occidental Churches celebrate their Liturgy! We should meditate and make ours the message Marie de l'Incarnation sends us through this letter.

Marie always kept her love for the Psalms and instilled the same love in those she counseled. Like the monks of the desert, the verses of the Psalms were always in her mouth as well as in her heart. She gave this advice to a friend: "Often repeat this verse of the Psalm, *Eructavit* to Jesus: '*Speciosus forma prae filiis hominum'*..." (Ps 44:3).[13] "I urged you to get a book of Psalms in French and Latin; there you will find the spiritual food which will satisfy your spiritual hunger with a satiety that does not disgust you, but continually fills the soul with loving thoughts of God."[14]

For Marie, the Psalms are expressing who God is, his attributes, and his love for us. They are the occasion for her to contemplate her beloved God. The following passage in *The Relation of 1654*, is very relevant:

---

[13] Ps 44(45):3: "You are the most handsome of men, fair speech has graced your lips, for God has blessed you forever."

[14] Marie de l'Incarnation, Letter to a friend, 1648, *Écrits*, IV, 218, quoted by Fernand Jetté, *op. cit.*, p. 87.

"In the psalms I saw his justice, his judgements, his grandeur, his love, his equity, his beauties, his magnificence, his generosity, and, finally, that he had (according to the sense of the Church, his spouse) 'well-shaped hands, full of hyacinths' and other fruits appropriate for revealing the fullness of purity to souls, his beloved ones. I saw that the goodness of this divine spirit had established me in green and fertile pasture which kept my soul so nourished that it overflowed and I could not keep silent."[15]

---

[15] Marie de l'Incarnation, *The Relation of 1654*, XXXIV, in Irene Ma-

No doubt, the reader has recognized Psalm 22(23). Marie de l'Incarnation gives the essentials of this magnificent Psalm, saying it in her own words, by heart, because it came from her inmost being like a second nature. She ruminated[16] it like a tasty meal and assimilated it in her prayer and language. She prays the Psalms as she breathes. They are continuously on her lips as well as in her mind and heart. Marie teaches what she lives. She says that the fervent soul will discover Christ's own sentiments in the Psalms, and this is the most accurate way of praising God. "What is more, if the soul remains faithful

---

honey, *op. cit.*, p. 101.

[16] Maria-Paul del Rosario Adria-zola, *La connaissance sprituelle chez Marie de l'Incarnation*, p. 284.

and sincere, it will imbibe their spirit, dictated as they were by the Spirit of God,"[17] who speaks to us.

Mary lives the Psalms; she feels with them and they express her feelings.

> "Sometimes my thoughts were concentrated on the purity of God and how all things declare his glory. The psalm 'The heavens declare the glory of God' (Ps 19) had an allure for me which pierced my heart and enraptured my spirit. 'Yes, yes, O my Love! 'Your testimonies are true; they are justified of themselves. They give witness to the foolish' (Ps 19:8).

---

[17] Marie de l'Incarnation, *The Relation of 1654, Écrits*, II, 167, referred to

Send me over the whole world to teach those who are ignorant of you."[18]

Marie desired that everyone know the things she experienced, and she wished everyone to taste the delights that her soul had experienced. So, during the recitation of the *"Laudate,"* she was in those transports which the Psalms evoked in her; she really lived the content of the Psalm.[19] Elsewhere she writes: "My spirit was so filled with all that was sung in choir, that day and night this formed my colloquy with my heavenly spouse."[20] Her life of

by Fernand Jetté, *op. cit.,* p. 87.

[18] Marie de l'Incarnation, *The Relation of 1654*, XXXIV, in Irene Mahoney, *op. cit.*, p. 102.

[19] *Idem,* p. 102.

[20] *Idem,* p. 102.

prayer nourished by the psalms sung during the Divine Office invades, "day and night," all her activities, even when she was at work.[21]

Let us see now how the Gospel affected her prayer. In the Gospel, the Spirit speaks to the person while reading. The words of Jesus are actual and can change those who accept them in their hearts. Let us still hear what she said about the Gospel: "The words spoken by the Incarnate Word which abound in the Gospel are, in my opinion, the fire and flame which He cast upon the earth and which continues to enkindle the pure of soul. What heart, however cold and unfeeling, is not enflamed

---

[21] *Idem*, p. 102.

while listening humbly and sincere-
ly to them."[22]

For Marie de l'Incarnation in
each word of the Scriptures abides a
divine efficaciousness. The words of
the Word printed themselves in her
heart as a law for her life. It was
through the Gospel that the Holy
Spirit dictated how she was to walk
toward God.[23]

Marie knew the New Testament
very well, and was able, with the
grace of the Holy Spirit, to connect
it with the Old Testament. Accord-

---

[22] Marie de l'Incarnation, Relations
d'oraison, *Écrits*, II, 97-98, quoted by
Fernand Jetté, *op. cit.*, p. 87. Cf. also
Maria-Paul del Rosario Adrazola, *La
connaissance spirituelle chez Marie de
l'Incarnation*, p. 279.

[23] Maria-Paul del Rosario Adrazola,
*La connaissance spirituelle chez Marie
de l'Incarnation*, p. 275-276.

ing to Maria-Paul del Rosario Adriazola, Marie de l'Incarnation had a
deep knowledge of the harmony
between the two Testaments. While
reading the Old Testament, her
mind was often carried toward the
images of the Gospel.[24] She was
aware of the fact that the events of
the Old Testament were signs and

---

[24] Marie de l'Incarnation writes: "Il
est arrivé que depuis ma profession
religieuse, le Seigneur a tenu mon esprit dans une douce contemplation des
beautés ravissantes de sa loi, et surtout
du rapport de la loi ancienne avec la loi
évangélique." *Écrits*, III, p. 49-50, in
Maria-Paul del Rosario Adrazola, *La
connaissance spirituelle chez Marie de
l'Incarnation*, p. 266.

["It has happened that since my religious profession, the Lord has kept
my mind in a gentle contemplation of
the ravishing beauties of his law, and
above all of the relationship of the old
law to the law of the Gospel."]

figures of Christ. And Marie de l'Incarnation also knew the eschatological meaning of the Scripture.[25] For instance, it is clear when Marie speaks about Christ as "the Way, the Truth and the Life." It is because Jesus is the Way that Mary had a continual tendency to follow Him always and higher. She said to Jesus: "You are my Life," because she experienced that He was for her soul "a life and a nourishing food," making her participate in eternal life already.[26] The words of Jesus are for her "spirit and life": "Everything He says is spirit and life in me."[27]

---

[25] Maria-Paul del Rosario Adrazola, *op. cit.*, p. 266.

[26] *Idem*, p. 266.

[27] Marie de l'Incarnation, *Écrits*, II, p. 461-462, quoted by Maria-Paul del Rosario Adrazola, *op. cit.*, p. 280.

Among the other books of the Bible which nourished her prayer was the Song of Songs. For her, this inspired poem was the best expression of her experience of her mystical marriage.[28] In *The Relation of 1654*, she writes that, after this mystical experience, she read the Song of Songs. She affirms that this sacred book corresponds most accurately to her personal experience. It has a deeper echo in her than simple words can cause.[29]

---

[28] Maria-Paul del Rosario Adrazola, *op. cit.*, p. 262.

[29] Marie de l'Incarnation writes: "Depuis ce temps-là, j'ai lu le Cantique des Cantiques dans l'Écriture Sainte. Je ne puis rien dire qui y ait plus de rapport, mais le fond expérimental fait bien d'autres impressions que ce que les paroles sonnent." *Écrits* II, p. 261. ["Since then, I have read the Song of Songs in Sacred Scripture. I cannot say

Marie de l'Incarnation had assimilated the Song of Songs so well that, during her novitiate, she was able, not only to pray and meditate on it, but to explain it with much unction to the other novices. While Marie was an assistant to the Mistress of Novices, she was asked by her to explain some passages of Holy Scripture to the novices. It happened that, while she was talking about the "Hail Mary," her "spirit was completely swept away." And from the explanation of the "Hail Mary," she quite naturally quoted

---

anything more about it, but the experimental background makes many more impressions than how the lyrics sound."] This quotation is taken from Maria-Paul del Rosario Adrazola, *op. cit.*, p. 262.

the Song of Songs.[30] It is interesting
to read that passage of the *Écrits*
because it shows how Marie de
l'Incarnation was filled with the
Song of Songs, so that she used it
very simply to comment on other
passages of the Bible.

> "It was concerning these
> words: 'and blessed is the
> fruit of thy womb.' This
> brought to mind that passage
> of the Holy Scripture in
> which Our Lord is the 'corn
> of the elect and wine bring-
> ing forth virgins' (Zec 9:17).
> I had to stop and let the Spir-
> it have his will with me or, to
> put it better, simply to en-
> dure what was happening in

---

[30] Marie de l'Incarnation, *The Relation of 1654*, XXXVIII, in Irene Ma-

my soul. Concerning this 'wine' there came to me a passage from the Song, 'My beloved is a cluster of grapes to me' (Song 1:13). I saw him as this corn. I saw him as the nourishment of our souls in the Blessed Sacrament, crushed like the grapes in the winepress of the cross, thus producing that wine out of which virgins spring."[31]

This quotation shows how her spiritual life is one. In her spirituality, the Word of God is related to the Eucharist. Her prayer takes its sap from the roots of Holy Scripture

---

honey, *op. cit.*, p. 110.

[31] Marie de l'Incarnation, *The Relation of 1654*, XXXVII, in Irene Mahoney, *op. cit.*, p. 110.

and the Liturgy. In her prayer, the Word of God, heard during the divine Office and the Eucharist are intimately woven to form one unique prayer. There is no dichotomy between her prayer of "day and night" and her prayer in the Church.

There is no separation between her teachings and her life of prayer. Marie de l'Incarnation notes the capacity she had to switch from concrete issues to the Word of God as if the Word of God were filling her mind and her heart. The following lines stress her capacity to relate everything in daily life to the Word of God. In beginning of her instruction, she used to read to her novices and the sisters the little *Catechism of the Council of Trent* or that of Cardinal Bellarmine. When after speaking of some article of faith, she would turn to questions of morality. She was amazed at the number of relevant passages of Holy Scripture which would come to her mind. She could not remain silent, for she had to obey the Spirit who possessed her.[32] Father Jetté notes that the "leaning on the Scriptures became a habit with her."[33] Marie de l'Incarnation expresses the connection existing between the way she had to settle daily concrete problems of exterior life, and her knowledge and familiarity with the Word of God in her interior life. She writes: "The knowledge Our Lord has granted me concerning Holy Scripture came to me at prayer and has helped

---

[32] *Ibid.*, p. 111.

[33] Fernand Jetté, *op. cit.*, p. 87.

greatly to order both my interior and exterior life."[34]

After these passages, it is obvious that Holy Scripture was a major influence in the spirituality of Marie de l'Incarnation. She affirms that her knowledge of the Scriptures is not the fruit of intellectual efforts and systematic studies. She was given this knowledge of Holy Scripture by Jesus, not while reading it but praying it (in French, *pendant l'oraison*).[35] The knowledge she obtains through Holy Scripture is a "*connaissance savoureuse*"[36] which

---

[34] *Ibid.*, p. 87-88.

[35] The French word "*oraison*" seems to be more precise than the English word "prayer" which is too general to express the nuances when we speak about prayer.

[36] Maria-Paul del Rosario Adrazola, *op. cit.*, p. 262-263 and 71-79 "*Science savoureuse*" is "*Sapida scientia*" accord-

illuminates and satisfies the soul's hunger by its "*suavité nourrissante,*"[37] and gives her living. Marie was aware of the "*grâce de sapience*"[38] which made her able to understand and preach the mysteries of faith in a coherent way.[39]

---

ing to the teaching of Sirach (6:23): "For discipline is like her name." *The New American Bible*, in footnotes, says that "discipline" means "wisdom" (*musar* in Hebrew). The French translation given by Maria-Paul del Rosario Adriazola is: "*La sagesse de la doctrine est conforme à son nom.*"

[37] These words of Marie of the Incarnation mean that the sweetness of the Divine science she received from Jesus through the Holy Spirit nourished her soul.

[38] "Grace of tasting the Word of God" should be an approximate translation of the "*grâce de sapience*".

[39] Maria-Paul del Rosario Adrazola, *op. cit.*, p. 79: "[...] *Marie sera profon-*

Her spiritual life is completely integrated; her knowledge of God as well as her "day and night" prayer to God are one with her familiarity with the Holy Scripture and the Eucharist.

In the following part, I will present some aspects of the second source of Marie de l'Incarnation's prayer, the Liturgy: prayer of the Church.

---

*dément consciente de "(porter) en (l')
âme une grâce de sapience", [...] qui lui
permet de comprendre et d'annoncer les
mystères de la foi d'une manière cohé-
rente."* ["[...] Mary will be deeply
aware of "(carrying) in (the) soul a
grace of sapience," which enables it to
understand and announce the mysteries of the faith in a coherent way."]

The Second Source of Marie de l'Incarnation's Prayer:

The Liturgy: Prayer of the Church

In the first part, we saw that the essence of Marie de l'Incarnation's prayer was the Word of God. The Holy Scripture was the food that nourished and united her soul to the most Holy Trinity.[40] Neverthe-

---

[40] Marie de l'Incarnation, *The Relation of 1654*, XXXIII, in Irene Mahoney, *op. cit.*, p. 99-100. She writes:

less, we can ask where and when was Marie in contact with the Word of God. The answer seems to be:

"One day at evening prayer, just as the signal had been given to begin, I was kneeling in my place in choir when a sudden inner transport ravished my soul. Then the three Persons of the Most Holy Trinity manifested themselves again through the words of the adorable Word incarnate: "If anyone loves me, my Father will love him; we will come to him and make our dwelling with him" (Jn 14:23). I then felt the effects of these divine words and the action of the three divine Persons in me more strongly than ever before. These words, by penetrating me with their meaning, brought me both to understand and to experience. Then the Most Holy Trinity, in its unity, took my soul to itself like a thing which already belonged to it, and which it had itself made capable of this divine imprint and the effects of his divine action."

when she participated in the Liturgy of the Church especially during the Divine Office and the Eucharist.

The Divine Office

Vocal prayers were very difficult for her, especially after the grace of her spiritual marriage in 1627.[41] She writes:

> "I found it very hard to say vocal prayers. I would no sooner begin my beads, thinking of the meaning of the words, when my spirit would be lost in God. I was obliged to stop or to say it at different times, whenever I had the opportunity. It was

---

[41] Fernand Jetté, *The Spiritual Teaching of Mary of the Incarnation*, p. 90.

the same with the Office of the Blessed Virgin."[42]

When she entered the Ursuline Order, by obedience to God's Will expressed in the Rule, she performed her exercises with more fervor, even if it was an effort for her.[43] In 1661, she writes to her son Claude: "The psalms are the only vocal prayers I can say, even the rosary of obligation is difficult for me."[44] Marie

---

[42] Marie de l'Incarnation, *Relation of 1654, Écrits*, II, 260, quoted by Fernand Jetté, *The Spiritual Teaching of Mary of the Incarnation*, p. 72.

[43] Fernand Jetté, *The Spiritual Teaching of Mary of the Incarnation*, p. 90-91.

[44] Marie de l'Incarnation, Letter to her son, September 25, 1670, *Lettres*, II, 474, in Fernand Jetté, *The Spiritual Teaching of Mary of the Incarnation*, p. 91.

took the opportunity for a few moments of silence, while the opposite choir was singing a verse, to compose her own prayer in order to have an intimate conversation with God. She writes:

> "While the psalms are being chanted in choir […] and the other side is chanting its verse, I converse freely with Our Lord about the meaning of the words, or else I follow the inspiration He gives me, when the verse is on our side, I pass from the interior to the exterior act; thus harmonizing the two, I do not leave His divine majesty for a moment.
>
> "Nevertheless, while attending to the singing, I do not feel this intimacy with

Our Lord as much as when the other choir is chanting. My spirit participates all the same. In one, I am left free to speak interiorly, whereas in the other, I am not as conscious of what is taking place within me because of the necessity of using my voice."[45]

The Divine Office was the opportunity for her to be more united to Jesus and, also, to receive from Jesus a better understanding of the Holy Scripture as she says in *The Relation of 1654*: "[...] my spirit [...] was more withdrawn than ever from things of the earth and drawn to-

---

[45] Marie de l'Incarnation, *Relation of 1633, Écrits*, I, 337, in Fernand Jetté, *The Spiritual Teaching of Mary of the Incarnation*, p. 91.

ward religious virtue and the Divine Office, where Our Lord bestowed on me a sweet and nourishing understanding of the Holy Scripture."[46] The Divine Office is the prayer in which she sees and tastes how God good is (Ps 34:9).[47]

---

[46] Marie de l'Incarnation, *The Relation of 1654*, XXXIV, in Irene Mahoney, *op. cit.*, p. 101.

[47] Maria-Paul del Rosario Adrazola, *La connaissance spirituelle chez Marie de l'Incarnation*, p. 281. This Author writes: "La parole de Dieu est ici 'une nourriture céleste'. Cela fut le cas tout particulièrement à l'Office divin. Dans ce domaine, c'est l'Esprit saint qui est le grand 'Maître intérieur'. Il explique les Écritures, car c'est lui qui les a inspires." (Cf. *Écrits*, II, p. 492). Le Saint Esprit lui fait expérimenter leur contenu (*Ibid.*, p. 268; *MI Correspondance*, p. 342, 748)). ["In this area, it is the Holy Spirit who is the great interior Master. He explains the Scriptures because he inspired them (Cf. *Écrits*, The

In the first part of the present research, we saw how the Psalms were
the Incarnation of knowledge of
God for Marie. "While in choir I
heard in French what I was chanting in Latin."[48] This act of singing
soothed her and liberated her spirit,
and she was able, while singing the
Psalms, to contemplate "his justice,
his judgments, his grandeur, his
love, his equity, his beauties, his
magnificence, his generosity,"[49] "revealing the fullness of purity to
souls, his beloved ones."[50]

Maria-Paul del Rosario Adrazola,
in her book *La connaissance spiritu-*

Holy Spirit makes her experiment with
their content.")]

[48] Marie de l'Incarnation, *The Relation of 1654*, XXXIV, in Irene Mahoney, *op. cit.*, p. 101.

[49] *Ibid.*, p. 101.

[50] *Ibid.*, p. 101.

elle chez Marie de l'Incarnation, shows how Marie de l'Incarnation understood the meaning of the texts of Holy Scripture through a kind of "chewing" to extract form it its savor: it is the *ruminatio*, the constant "chewing," repeating the divine Words. Marie de l'Incarnation acquired this assimilated knowledge of the Psalms. It was through the Holy Spirit that she was granted this special grace to "see and taste" the spiritual realities.[51]

Moreover, according to the same Author, it is while praising God, during the Divine Office, that the prayer of Marie de l'Incarnation merges with the prayer of the Church and that her spiritual knowledge is transformed into real

---

[51] Maria-Paul del Rosario Adrazola, *La connaissance spirituelle chez Marie*

theology.[52] One can say that the prayer of Marie de l'Incarnation draws in the Liturgy of the Hours. Marie prays in the Church, with the Church, and for the Church when she is united so intimately with God while praying the Psalms. The Divine Office, as Jesus revealed it to Marie de l'Incarnation, is the summary of the praise of the two sisters: the earthly Church and the heavenly

---

de l'Incarnation, p. 283-284.

[52] *Ibid.*, p. 284. The Author writes: "C'est dans la louange de Dieu, à l'office divin, que la prière de Marie de l'Incarnation s'intègre dans la prière de l'Église et que sa connaissance spirituelle se transforme en véritable théologie." ["It is in the praise of God, in the divine office, that the prayer of Mary of the Incarnation is integrated into the prayer of the Church and that her spiritual knowledge is transformed into true theology."]

Church. According to Marie-Paul del Rosario Adriazola, the Liturgy, while purifying, projects us beyond ourselves into the light of God who tranfigures.[53] Marie's faith and love were fed by the Divine Office.

---

[53] Maria-Paul del Rosario Adrazola, *La connaissance spirituelle chez Marie de l'Incarnation*, p. 289.

The Author writes: "La prière est l'expression intime et spontanée de la certitude de la proximité de Dieu, de sa présence aimante en nous. Elle est l'expression personnelle de ce rapport ontologique avec Dieu. Car Dieu est venu habiter en nous par sa grâce. Nous sommes 'temples' de son Amour. Nous avons ainsi la possibilité de la reconnaissance de cette présence et l'obligation de répondre à cette grâce. La prière est un acquiescement profond, une adhésion silencieuse. Il y a, néanmoins, une prière exprimée qui se manifeste extérieurement. Or, l'excellence de l'Office divin, c'est qu'ici, et comme le Seigneur le révèle à

Marie de l'Incarnation, se résume la
louange des deux soeurs: l'Église terre-
stre et la céleste. La liturgie, en purifi-
ant, nous projette au-delà de nous-
mêmes dans la lumière de Dieu qui
transfigure. Une lumière qui graduel-
lement éclaire et resplendit, un 'touch-
er' qui façonne en nous, peu à peu, cet
'homme nouveau', recréé à l'image du
Christ. Grâce à la liturgie, nous
devenons cet 'homme vivant qui est la
gloire de Dieu', de saint Irénée." (*Adv.
Haer.* IV, 20) ["Prayer is the intimate
and spontaneous expression of the cer-
tainty of the closeness of God, of his
loving presence in us. It is the personal
expression of this ontological relationship with God. For God has come to
dwell in us by his grace. We are 'temples' of his Love. We thus have the pos-
sibility of the recognition of this presence and the obligation to respond to
this grace. Prayer is a deep acquies-
cence, a silent adhesion. There is, however, an expressed prayer that mani-
fests outwardly. Now, the excellence of
the Divine Office is that here, and as

The Eucharist

The Eucharist is the other table where Marie feeds her faith and love. She was opposed to the practice of her time in which was reserved Holy Communion only for those considered to be perfect. Marie de l'Incarnation, who personally met Saint Francis of Sales and read

---

the Lord revealed to Mary of the Incarnation, is summed up the praise of the two sisters: the earthly Church and the heavenly one. The liturgy, by purifying, projects us beyond ourselves into the light of God who transfigures. A light which gradually illuminates and shines, a 'touch' which shapes in us, little by little, this 'new man,' recreated in the image of Christ. Thanks to the liturgy, we become that 'living man who is the glory of God,' of Saint Irenaeus."]

his *Introduction à la vie dévote,*[54] is in complete accord with him in regard to his conviction that Holy Communion should be considered "as nourishment for the soul, not as a reward for virtue. This thrust toward more frequent Communion was […] of immense importance to Marie."[55]

Sister Irene Mahoney, in her Introduction to the *Selected Writings of Marie de l'Incarnation,* does not hesitate to affirm that it was in Marie's response to the Eucharist that she "shows herself most unique."[56] It was at a times when the reception of the Eucharist was reserved for those who merited it because of

---

[54] Marie de l'Incarnation, *Selected writings,* Edited by Irene Mahoney, O.S.U., *Introduction,* p. 21.

[55] *Ibid.,* p. 21.

their virtue. This sacrament was not considered as food for the weak and the hungry.[57] It is amazing that in such an atmosphere, Mary asked her director permission to receive daily Communion. For her, the Eucharist was "not a reward for the good but nourishment for those in need."[58] In *The Relation of 1654*, she stresses the effects of the Eucharist: "Communion always inclined me toward virtue and trust in the goodness of God." And she also writes in the same text: "The more I approached the sacraments, the more I desired them, for there I found life and goodness and a longing for prayer. I wanted everyone whom

---

[56] *Ibid.*, p. 22.

[57] *Ibid.*, p. 22.

[58] *Ibid.*, p. 22.

Our Lord let me encounter to experience this love."[59]

In the *Dictionnaire de spiritualité*, Fr. Éphrem Longpré does not hesitate to affirm that "Marie de l'Incarnation is among the first to rank as a Eucharistic Mystic."[60] To support his affirmation, he quotes A. Jamet: "For her, the Eucharist is above all the food of Christian life, principally in its higher form: a life

---

[59] Marie de l'Incarnation, *The Relation of 1654*, III, in Irene Mahoney, *op. cit.*, p. 44-45.

[60] Éphrem Longpré,. "Eucharistie et expérience mystique", in *Dictionnaire de spiritualité*, Paris, Beauchesne, 1961, col. 1611. "Marie de l'Incarnation est au premier rang des mystiques eucharistiques." ["Mary of the Incarnation is at the forefront of the Eucharistic mystics."]

of prayer.[61] That kind of idea was not popular, even among the theologians of her time."[62] According to Fr. Éphrem Longpré, *The Relation*

---

[61] To translate the French word "*oraison*". Cf. footnote 37.

[62] Fr. Éphrem Longpré, *loc. cit.*, quoting A. Jamet, *Écrits spirituels et historiques*, t. 1, Québec-Paris, 1919, p. 170, note a; cf. H. Cuzin, *Du Christ à la Trinité d'après l'expérience mustique de Marie de l'Incarnation*, Lyon, 1936, p. 92-99). "Pour elle, l'eucharistie est surtout l'aliment de la vie chrétienne, principalement sous sa forme la plus haute: la vie d'oraison. Pareille idée n'était pas courante, même chez les théologiens, à cette époque." [*From Christ to the Trinity according to the mystical experience of Mary of the Incarnation*: "For her, the Eucharist is above all the nourishment of Christian life, mainly in its highest form: the life of prayer. Such an idea was not common, even among theologians, at that time."]

of 1633 and *The Relation of 1654*
attest that, from the time of her
youth, her interior life grew and
reached summits through Eucharistic piety and an intense liturgical
life.[63] Waiting for her mystical marriage, which happened at Pentecost,
1627, she found her strength only
through daily communion.[64] She

---

[63] Ephrem Longpré, loc. cit., col.
1611. The Author of the article refers
to the *Écrits*, t. 1, p. 170-173; t. 2, p.
165, 167, 170-1723, 180. "Dès sa jeu-
nesse, sa vie intérieure se développe et
atteint les sommets par la piété eucha-
ristique et la vie liturgique intense."
["From her youth, her interior life developed and reached the summits
through Eucharistic piety and intense
liturgical life."]

[64] Cf. Ephrem Longpré, *loc. cit.,* col
1611. He refers to *Écrits*, t. 1, p. 153-
154. He also refers to J. Klein,
L'itinéraire mystique de la vénérable

said that it was in daily Communion that her soul finds relief. In this Communion, she knew that she possessed God's life. She found a new strength in the Eucharist. She said that, tired out by the services rendered to her neighbor and by her penances, her body recovered vigor through eating the divine bread. She obtained a new courage to begin anew what she would not have been able to do by her own natural strength.[65] It was during the cele-

---

mère Marie de l'Incarnation, Issoudun-Paris, 1938, p. 39-40.

[65] Marie de l'Incarnation, *Écrits*, t. 2, p. 222-223. "Le plus grand soulagement que l'âme trouve […] est dans la communion journalière, où elle est assurée qu'elle possède sa vie. […] Après toutes mes fatigues que je prenais pour le service du prochain, mon corps brisé de pénitences reprenait ses forces par la manducation

bration of the Eucharist as well as in its adoration that Marie received new strength and eminent graces.[66] Even when she was working for her brother-in-law on the wharf at Tours, she remained united to the

---

de ce divin pain et un nouveau courage pour recommencer tout de nouveau, ce que naturellement je n'aurais pu." In *Dictionnaire de Spiritualité*, col. 1612. ["The greatest relief that the soul finds [...] is in daily communion, where it is assured that it owns its life. [...] After all my fatigue that I took for the service of my Neighbors, my body, broken with penance, regained its strength through the manducation of this divine bread and new courage to start all over again, which naturally I would not have been able to."

[66] Éphrem Longpré, *loc. cit.*, col 1612. The Author refers to *Écrits*, t. 1, p. 171; t. 2, p. 233-236, p. 482. Cf. H. Cuzin, *op. cit.*, p. 71-74; cf. J. Klein, *op. cit.*, p. 62-66.

Christ she had received that morning in Holy Communion, the "sacrament of love"[67]

---

[67] Marie de l'Incarnation, *Écrits*, t. 1, p. 215: "Je ne saurais exprimer la force ni la douceur de l'union de mon âme avec Notre-Seigneur, principalement par la sainte communion. Et, c'était d'ordinaire après cette action que j'allais vaquer aux affaires de mon beau-frère, ni le bruit des rues, ni ce que j'avais à traiter avec les marchands, ni tous les soins dont j'étais chargée ne me pouvaient tirer de la liaison intérieure que j'avais avec la Divinité. Je me sentais remplie de l'unité de Dieu au fond de l'âme par le moyen de ce sacrement d'amour, et quoique j'en eusse la présence habituelle, c'était néanmoins d'une manière tout autre. Cela me faisait une faim continuelle de communier sans cesse, s'il m'eût été possible, parce que j'expérimentais que c'est là où l'on jouit vraiment de Dieu. [...]" ["I could not express the strength or the gentleness of the union of my soul with Our Lord, mainly through

Marie de l'Incarnation's burning love was given to her in Holy Communion each time she received Jesus in the Eucharist. This loving fire which united her so intimately to God often caused *"embrasse-*

---

holy communion. And, it was usually after this action that I would go about my brother-in-law's business, neither the noise of the streets, nor what I had to do with the merchants, nor all the care with which I was charged could not pull me out of the inner connection I had with Divinity. I felt filled with the oneness of God deep in my soul by means of this sacrament of love, and although I had the usual presence of it, it was nevertheless in a very different way. It made me continually hungry to receive Communion without ceasing, if it had been possible for me, because I experienced that this is where one truly enjoys God. […]"

ments"[68] during her activities and on the road.[69]

---

[68] *Embrassement* may be translated by "embracing."

[69] Marie de l'Incarnation, *Écrits*, t. 1, p. 352-353: "Toutes les fois que j'ai fait la sainte communion, [...] j'ai si fort senti l'amour de Notre-Seigneur en ce divin sacrement que je ne puis dire tout ce qu'a senti mon cœur [...] C'est un feu amoureux qui fait que l'âme expérimente les paroles de Notre-Seigneur: Apprenez de moi que je suis doux et humble de cœur (Mt 11,29). J'ai pâti une si grande paix, mais quelquefois plus qu'à l'ordinaire, que je la puis exprimer, et ensuite de cela j'ai été si fort liée à Dieu, allant et venant à mes actions, que quelquefois mes grands embrassements se font en chemin." ["Every time I have made Holy Communion [...] I have felt the love of Our Lord so strongly in this divine sacrament that I cannot say all that my heart has felt [...] C t is a loving fire which causes the soul to experience the words of Our Lord: Learn from me that

In regard to what we have seen above, we may agree with Father Éphrem Longpé who concludes his article on Marie de l'Incarnation asserting that her witness is unique in the mystical literature of the Church.

I am meek and humble of heart (Mt 11:29). I have suffered such a great peace, but sometimes more than usual, that I can express it, and after that I have been so strongly linked to God, coming and going to my actions, that sometimes my great embraces are made on the way."]

Conclusion

According to what has been written, we already saw that it was in the Liturgy of the Church, during the celebration of the **Mass** as well as during the **Divine Office**, that Marie was continually nourished by the **Word of God**, made flesh for our salvation and given as supernatural food in the **Eucharist**. The **Liturgy** has a central place in the spiritual life of Marie de l'Incarnation. It unifies it, creating essential links between the Word of God sung and proclaimed during the Divine Office and the Mass on one hand, and, on the other hand, the Word made flesh, received with his Body, Soul, Blood and Divinity in Holy Communion. This vital union of the two in Marie is the work of the Holy Spirit as we have been able to observe while reading Marie's *Relations* and *Écrits*.

I may conclude then, that the spiritual life of Marie de l'Incarnation is vitally linked to the life of her Mother, the Church. She herself justly affirms that she is "**the daughter of the Church**." She writes: "This is a great consolation to the soul who feared being deluded, for now it sees that everything that has happened to it falls within the faith of the Church. It experiences profound peace and great happiness to

be the daughter of the Church."[70]
The piety of Marie, her spirituality,
her theology are totally conformed
to the teaching of the Scripture and
the Catholic Church. We find in the
spirituality of Marie de l'Incarnation the characteristics which au-
thenticate its Christian value:[71]

1. It is corporate and ecclesial,
   organically united to the faith
   and the life of the Church.

2. It is scriptural, nourished by
   the Holy Scripture to believe
   and worship.

---

[70] Marie de l'Incarnation, *The Relation of 1654*, XIX, in Irene Mahoney,
op. cit., p. 76.

[71] Fr. Marc-Daniel Kirby's *Spiritual
Theology* class at Holy Apostles College
& Seminary, Classnotes, February 8,
1999.

3. It is sacramental and liturgical: the Eucharist is its center.

Therefore, we are justified to
conclude that Marie de l'Incarnation teaches us the way to **see** and
love God. Ending this research, I
quote a passage of *The Relation of
1654* which expresses very well her
desire to see and love God:

"The soul sings to him: 'Who
will help me find you, my
Beloved, so that I will kiss
you and embrace you at leisure and give you the juice of
my pomegranates to eat?'
(Song 8:1-2). It wishes to
find him beyond all the aspects of his majesty which
make him so formidable and
thus she says, 'Flee, my Be-

loved, go among the spices.' Go among the cherubim, to those who alone can bear your light. Then come, O my Love, that I may overflow within you, by an exchange of love – so far as my lowliness permits and your love allows. 'This is why I have longed to see you, my little brother, who sucked at my mother's breasts,' O adorable Word Incarnate, 'may I embrace you at my leisure and may no one be scandalized,' for you have made yourself as you are for this purpose and this is why I long for you (Song 8:14,1). **Thus, the soul is not prompted by curiosi-**

**ty to see but is insatiable in
its desire to love.**"[72]

This text helps us to discover the burning heart of Marie de l'Incarnation who invites each of us to desire not only to see but to love God. We must not forget that all the things Marie de l'Incarnation said to us through her writings does not come from her, but from the Spirit who led her to do so.[73] Finally let us sing with her:

"MAY HE BE
ETERNALLY BLESSED."[74]

---

[72] Marie de l'Incarnation, *The Relation of 1654*, XIX, in Irene Mahoney, *op. cit.*, p. 77.

[73] *Ibid.*, p. 77.

[74] *Ibid.*, p. 77.

Epilogue

Having finished the French translation of this English edition of *The two sources of Marie de l'Incarnation's prayer*, I have the impression of leaving behind a friend with whom I have lived many intimate hours in a *tete-a-tete* during which she shared with me her most intimate secrets of her love of her divine Spouse.

I also have the impression of having benefited from an immense privilege by receiving the confidences of this extraordinary woman. My meetings with her were for the purpose of discovering in a very superficial way – I admit it – her life of prayer, her life of intimacy with

God. The work has made me think of certain journalists who have extensively interviewed eminent personalities such as the Pope or certain heads of state. From this long meeting, I developed an admiration for this woman who knew how to unite to a high degree the contemplative life and the active life.

Marie Guyart, young child, marriageable girl, wife, mother, entrepreneur, construction site manager, teacher, polyglot, linguist, dictionary writer, diplomat, mistress of novices, community superior, bursar, painter, embroiderer, musician, player of both the viola and the harpsichord, composer of songs and pieces for the harpsichord, editor of *Relations*, writer of nearly three thousand letters—throughout this hectic life, she remained in intimate contact with her divine Spouse. She *breathed* God in all her actions.

We can say of this great mystic that she kept both feet firmly planted in reality in the service of humanity where she was active and in the service of her Heavenly Lord and Spouse who accompanied her and supported her in everything and everywhere.

Historians recognize that she played a major role in the creation of New France, which was already called "Canada". How brave! what insight! What audacity in her participation in the organization and proper functioning of the young colony established on the narrowing of the great river, a narrowing that the Hurons called "Kébec".

As for Saint Marie de l'Incarnation, everything could be transformed into a prayer, so I end with a prayer:

> *Thanks, Lord, for giving me the grace of living long hours of research and reflection with your spouse, Marie Guyart, Saint Marie de l'Incarnation. She encourages me by her example to intensify my life of intimate union with you, Jesus, and to be, like her, attentive to the needs of the people you put on my path. Amen!*

And I pray to Saint Marie of the Incarnation to obtain for all people who will discover, on reading this book, the main lines of her spirituality, the favor of intensifying their life of union with the Lord Jesus, truly alive and actively present in their daily lives.

SAINT MARY

OF THE INCARNATION,

PRAY FOR US!

Bibliography

Adriozola, Maria-Paul del Rosario Adriazola, *La connaissance spirituelle chez Marie de l'Incarnation*. Paris, Cerf, 1989. 407 pages.

Giguère, Herman, "Des quais de la Loire aux rives du St-Laurent" in *Selon sa Parole*, vol.12, numéro 5, 15 mai 1986. On the internet:

http://www.diocesequebec.qc.ca

Jetté, Fernand, O.M.I., *The Spiritual Teaching of Mary of the Incarnation*, translated by Mother M. Herman, O.S.U. New York, Sheed and Ward, 1962. 180 pages.

Fournet, A. "Ven. Marie de l'Incarnation" in *Catholic Encyclopedia*, 1913. Electronic version, 1997, by New Advent, Inc.

l'Incarnation, Marie de. *The Autobiography of Venerable Marie of the Incarnation, O.S.U., Mystic and Missionary.* Translated by Fr. John J. Sullivan, S.J. Chicago, Loyola University Press, 1964. 218 pages.

Kirby, Marc-Daniel, O.Cist., *Spiritual Theology*, Personal notes. Course given in Holy Apostles College and Seminary, Cromwell, CT, 2nd term, 1998-1999.

Longpré, Éphrem, "Eucharistie et expérience mystique" in *Dictionnaire de spiritualité*, col. 1611-1613. Paris, Beauchesne, 1961.

Mahoney, Irene, O.S.U., editing *Marie of the Incarnation, Selected Writings*, Coll. "Sources of American Spirituality". New York, Paulist Press, 1989. 286 pages.

www.ingramcontent.com/pod-product-compliance
Lightning Source LLC
Chambersburg PA
CBHW060142050426
42448CB00010B/2259